Shattered Thoughts

Scott Shaw

Buddha Rose Publications

ISBN: 1-877792-44-6
ISBN-13: 9781877792441

Library of Congress Control Number:
2009924876

First Edition: 2007

The collections of poetry presented in this volume
are derived from some of the previously published
poetry books written by Scott Shaw. The title of
each chapter details the book that the poetry
originally was published within.

10 9 8 7 6 5 4 3 2 1

Printed in the United States of America

Shattered
Thoughts

the poetry of Scott Shaw

Table of Contents

Chapter 1

SCREAM
Southeast Asia and the Dream

8

1

awoke to a pounding rhythm
a movement in a plastic vision
I wake to her asian eyes
staring into mine

no, I don't want your love
my head it hurts too much
no, I don't need your love
I can buy it anywhere
on any street in town
yes, I have compassion
compassion for the fools
yes, I made a promise
a promise like all of those before
words that means so little
you can say anything
and it will mean nothing
my words they are just the same

and tomorrow it never comes
so don't talk about it to me
and today it doesn't mean anything
I just don't want to
hear about it anymore

kiss me/love me/hold me
let it last as long as it will last
leave the promises
for the family-men/the businessmen
the prophets and the preachers
they have something to offer
not me
give me cold hard love
cold hard cash

cold hard life
leading to cold hard death
for that is where
all the promises go anyway

2

a taste of the red wine
pour it into my glass
a kiss with your lips
if you please
tickets to the passages
into the sanctuary
of the realms of the night

      lust, they say I look for lust
      I prefer to believe
      that I seek enlightenment
      worshipping the goddess
      who is bound by human form

and the waves of her body
pound onto me
like the surf
in the southeast asian sun
and her promises
they mean nothing to me
I listen
but words are all that I hear

      so give me my drug of choice
      keep the speeches
      for those who like to listen to the lies
      for me,
      I know that words mean nothing
      action speaks all
      and what you can show me
      is worth more than
      anything you could say to me
      please show me here,
      with your body

yes, right there
place it upon mine

3

a dark kiss of victory
like the black curse
of the Goddess of Siam

black is the night
black like her hair
fading into a golden body
that melted into mine

       heat
       it pounds down upon me
       passion
       it dances on my soul
       and her love
       it lasted only a moment
       a moment
       well, that was long enough

4

I drink a glass of suicide
redemption in a cup
a lady she lays next to me
I do not know her name
skin dark/hair black
burned by the southeast asian sun
and if I were any more than her
or if the price, it was not so high
then I would take her away with me
run in any direction
where the night
would not hold our souls so bound
but she and I
no, we will never be given a second chance
for destinies hold is far too tight
so, I kiss her
one time for the moment
I kiss her one time for the dream
I kiss her one time
for no reason at all
I kiss her
and wonder why life has let us go astray

so feed me what you have to give me
I will take it
in any form that it comes
the night time is for whispers
the day time is for screams
spread your love disease upon me
leave me no room for escape

5

red wine touches my lips
her golden body touches my body
and the heat it pounds on my soul

a moment for the illusion
a moment cast only to the memory
and it was love that lasted forever
forever, it was only a day

the ceiling fan rotates
the vision of the sunlight in burma
is fading
the green flowered wall papered walls
turn to gray

the fan turns
I turn
she turns
covered with sweat our bodies merge
all rotates/as my head it spins
as forever is only a moment
and the goddess
has once again stolen my soul

6

a bangkok morning screams to me
awoken by the chao praya ships
that move on the river below
her essence it cries out to me
wailing to wipe away her tears

but looking into her morning eyes
all I can see is a reason to leave
the heat, outside
the heat, inside
it never is cool here
never, never, never
this heat, it is killing me

and when all the dreams
have been desired
and all the desires
have lived then died
and when the love
showed me no answers
then the only conclusion
is to walk away
just walk away
leave to nowhere/leave to nothing
nothing never means anything, anyway
no reason to return
walk out into the heat
the fierce heat/the pouring heat/the pounding heat
like a rabid awakening
screaming for the dream
all there is here is the heat
hot
life here, it is so hot

7

I met her on an airplane
jakarta to singapore
first kiss on a beach
at sunset
down in old mexico

maybe I am just getting older
maybe it is that I
just don't care
maybe it is that in my memory
she just looked better
maybe I am just far too tainted
to get excited
about experiences such as these

so leave the sunset kisses for the movies
leave the semi-babes
for those who like illusion
leave the first loves
for the children
just give me a drink
just give me the cold hard night
where a first kiss
is not the only kiss
and the word, no
never comes to mind
let me live the southeast asian nights
where any dream is have-able
and anything that is wanted
is placed directly in my hand

8

a knock
in slices its way through the silence
slowly I rise
in the casual
semi darkness
open my hotel room door
the city of hong kong pounds
to a thursday night time rhythm
the city/the night/the illusion below
enter
older than I thought she would be
eyes, a bit wilder
than their chinese origin should allow
she steps in
my meditation for the evening
my vessel of love
a passage to passion
paid for
like all relationships
all good things
love that is bought and sold

in-house/of-house masseuse
oh, promise me your love forever
tell me that you will never go away

keep my robe on, she says to me
as she pulls back the blankets on the bed
and lays me down
upon clean white sheets

white, it is for saints
this room is for the sinner
paint it black, if you please

I on my stomach
her hands upon my back
through the hotel room robe
thin white line/thin white lies
as the questions of purpose
plays a song in my mind
an answer to seek/a need to fulfill
what is the actual
name of this game
are we going to get down to it
or what

she turns me over
her eyes find their way
to my pleasure zone
as my semi exposed body is revealed
a notice of her glance/a smile
from her lips
her hands again moving
everywhere to nowhere

and like the perfect paid for passion
like, how could I keep it down
hands placed
oh so precisely/move me into the mood
the juices
they get a-flowing/the river rising
a promise/the price
it moves up, $700.00 US
and like all of the best
who get you where you want to be
and then later tell you the cost
it could only be paid
what is money for anyway

she raises her
white surgical steel dress
like a nurse/like a nun
before I could even think/say a word
it was in/she was on
on to off
and all the purposes in between
leave it to some uncensored poet
leave it to your dreams

her body wasn't all in full view
the way I like it
I mean, I generally like to see
what I'm having
my vision was blocked
b u t I rolled her over
and for a second
it was in sight/insight
and for all the perfection
of this pagan moment
I could not help but fall in love

the dirty deed done
off and on her way out
come again tomorrow, I asked
but I never saw her again

and for all of those possible loves
that you glance at
see for a passing moment
wish for
but they are gone
and never seen again
for all those dreams
that you only wish
could have happened

a paid price
is worth it all
to taste/to touch/to feel

and love, it is so easy
stabbed down deep
like a knife
in the heart
a meditation
it leads to enlightenment
mine was complete that night

9

hotel wall painted off white
love wrapped in the arms of strangers
call it a foal's passion
a promise for a price
for when you want to play
you know that you have got to pay

      the dreams spin
      plastered hard
      against an off white wall
      as the ceiling fan turns
      as we turn
      as the earth turns
      all counter clockwise
      and the nights
      live on forever
      screaming for the dream

a promised passion/a promised price
and love, what does it mean anyway

      so hand me the lies
      that out live the truths
      give me an illusion to hold onto
      and when the greatest illusion
      is seen to be
      that there is no illusion at all
      then the Buddha
      will have been understood
      and life, it will tick on

      tick-tock
      fuck the clock

10

the night cries of mystery
it screams for the dream
the day
all it does is whisper
far too silent/far too soft
in the wisdom it is trying to convey

       and the sun bleeds
       its warm presence onto me
       awaking the dawn

       from one side/to the other side
       let me know its name

and all the wizards, they lie
and the sorcerers, they cry
and the holy,
they know nothing at all
for their knowledge it is lost
in what is/in what has to be
what it is/what it ain't
and as for the sinners
they are the knowers

       sin, from the ancient hebrew,
       to merge

dish me up a plate of illusion
for I have nothing left to lose
kiss me with the lips of desire
a goddess in any form
give me a night to experience truth
the kind the holy will never know
hand me a cup of redemption

suicide in a glass
let me live among those who know
the knowledge of the night

11

night time falls
as it tends to do
love
she wants to give hers to me

the light is dim
long black hair falling
it caresses my face
I look up
see her closed asian eyes
as her wet lips meet mine

I have to re-close my eyes
for it is all too much
like a fucking movie

kiss me/love me
yeah, sure
but let's leave all this melodrama
for the soap operas upon the screen
I prefer it raw
I prefer it hard
dirty and blatant
no prisoners taken
none looked for

then what is known
is known
what is felt
is felt
and the romance
it is left for the dreamers
who believe in all that bullshit

12

come over here
for I am tired
lay in my arms
lay upon my couch
let your asian eyes
look into mine
and talk to me of love
talk to me of marriage
talk to me of all of those things
that do not mean anything
at all
lay w/ me
love w/ me
kiss me good night

13

a longing child like face
of abstinence
a glance back over the shoulder
I left without wanting to leave
love/time
it is all gone

the stories they have all been told
see them upon any T.V./movie screen
but the love in the heart
the knife in the stomach
it is what has meaning
not the momentary dreams
of actors who lie
some distant place/some distant scene

there I was walking
there she was standing
her black hair blowing in the wind
her asian eyes transfixed upon my soul
and the sun shed its light onto me
as the lies spun in my mind
and the gods
they offered me no answer
to the question
"do you still love me?"
as I walked away

14

letter from thailand
"won't you come back to me."
come back/go back
it never seems to be the same

now, I could go there
lay in her asian arms
do nothing but let the days pass
the nights scream
and live in the poetry

but going back
is just like it sounds
it doesn't mean
or add up to anything

I've tried it before
even with her
but the memory
is always better
than the cold pagan cut
of the knife of life

the truth is bought
the lies come out
and all the words of love
didn't mean anything at all

so thanks
but no thanks
next time I'm there
I will just look the other way

15

disco dolly for rent/for hire
southeast asia
by geographical bounds
white lies/white eyes
it buys me an easy ticket into paradise

wet my lips
the drink does flow
beauty condensed
in an alcoholic form
skin so golden/hair so black
in her eyes
i see a green card/a dollar sign
my two tickets
to promised passion in the burning heat of this night

leave the vows
for the fools who call themselves
the family men
I prefer this
a different dream
with every passing passion
a different chance in every dance

> a lie
> it equals
> all that I can take
> a lie
> and I never need to speak a word

dream night princesses
they simply apply for it
the color of my skin,
my hair/my eyes of blue

16

the night air is warm
in the radio station
and we are left alone
the music,
we place it on tape
to be played tomorrow

tomorrow is always another day

so we sit back, she and I
and we dog down

peachy is her name
the princess of bangkok radio
pichitra on her U.S, passport
named by the queen of thailand
no lie

but now she has developed a passion
it is a unbreakable spell
it leads her from one day to the next
pong kow as it is called
powder white

one minute spreads to the other
for soon she must be home
children to take care of
a Thai husband
who she doesn't love to love
but for now
the moment is simple
a time in which
I watch her eyes spin

her eyes spin/my eyes spin
an embrace in illusion
an embrace of the best kind
as she reveals to me
all of her secrets
and all of the powers of the powder white

here and now it is all that matters
bangkok radio simply pays the bills
the bills for a white princess in a golden land
whose desire of illusion
sends her into the best
of what bangkok has to offer
white power ma

hello bangkok
this is your nighttime D.J.
rock'n hollywood scott
and my good friend peachy tells me
that we are going
to pick up the pace here a little bit
with a band from my home town of L.A.
but remember bangkok
when you wanta' play you gotta' pay

17

a man, a bangkok man stands
he stands hanging one
on the side of the deserting street

a lady, a bangkok lady
she is waiting/awaiting something
I know not what

the neon lights reflect in both of their skins
displaying/decaying
telling a story
that can never be fathomed
never truly be understood
only seen/only witnessed

he is dressed in gray pants
a dark blue shirt
his eyes are hidden
deeply into the pole

she has long black hair
a long yellow dress
and stares into some distance
that my western eyes
can never see

I pass him/I pass her

he is vacant
his back turned to me

her face
radiates the reflecting colors
pink/red/blue

all of the bangkok night

him, I have no feeling for
her, I could love
if given the chance

pictures and scenes
and all the figures in a dream
they all add up to the same thing
nothing
not anything at all

18

scalded by the heat of the bangkok night
touched once too hard
once too often
and love it proved nothing to me
loved/lost
loved again
but lust handed me the illusion
a dream worth living forever

and so few could know her
as I have known her
goddess green
bangkok night

and so few could have lived her
like I have loved her
siam dream
buddha gold
and all being had/all being held
I run from her/I run back to her
the price my soul
a price so high…

Chapter 2

Suicide Slowly

1

"what are you up to?"

"suicide slowly."

> for all of those
> who hold onto the dream
> or wish for
> the ultimate kiss of death
>
> for everything that is worth having
> but the first step in getting it
> is just too hard to take
> for all the tears that are cried
> to no one else's ears
> and when tomorrow's promises
> mean nothing more than today's lies
>
> just kiss me goodbye
>
> I choose suicide slowly

2

awh…

you're not even an artist
if you haven't spent
four or five christmas' alone
have a few line on your face
cried yourself to sleep
more than a few times
and walked down too many streets alone

alone, while others walked hand-in-hand

and if you think artists have women
no way
you're not even close
until you have spent more nights alone
than sleeping
bound and embraced
engulfed and intertwined

an artist
you don't want to be that

3

a girl
she is waiting for me
waiting
on the other side of town
waiting and wanting
desiring and needing
over there
on the other side of town

     and yes, we are world's apart

     to know me
     is to love
     so I have heard it said
     said and spoken
     to know her
     is to love her
     but loving her
     it is the death of me

     sanctuary in a glass/suicide in a cup

and her love
it runs through my veins
like a drug
a piercing poison/fierce addition
stringing my soul along

     and with nowhere left to run
     no one left to run to
     I cross the city/I cross the town
     I fall into her arms
     and for a moment my addition
     Is met/fulfilled

to know her
is to love her
to know her
is killing me

      sublime obsession
      in a broken world
      so supreme

I love her
I do not want to love her

4

sitting in the fading sun
a cup of *java* in my hand
a brief hollow/hallowed wind blows
as I stare into my own disparity
looking down the throat
of my own confusion
my inability to conform

and yes,
I have a million things to do
a million and one
if you please
and money,
well no,
I don't have any
they, the world
tells me that I should get a job

      thank you but no thank you
            someone has to die still dreaming

and yes, I still hold onto the dream
as I wait in this afternoon
for a miracle to come down

      die to dream
          dream to die

waiting w/ a cup of the *java*
in my hand

      as a hollow/hallowed wind
         gentle blows

5

scream
and there is no one there to hear it
is it a scream at all?

die
it touched a fantasy deep inside
but it was gone

live
when/where/why/how

drink
I think so
it is easier that way

6

the sun in my eyes
the wind cools its blow
the sound of the city
pounds in my head
I look
and there is no place
left to run

      the nighttime it is for whispers
          the daytime it is for screams

      and the lost
      are left intermixed
      with the living
      pretending to be
      but not being the same

7

the red wine flows like blood
the blood that poured out of her veins

      I was not thee to see it
      given the chance
      I would have walked the other way

drink me into drunken stupor
her passion was my promise
a promise
I never could have kept

drink me down
like this glass I finish
finish too fast
the fact to finish
my taste buds
they have become so numb

      I could have loved her
      didn't really want to
      didn't really know how
      I told her I did anyway

      words, they just don't mean a thing
            not anything at all

a bottle finished
another bottle down
a life gone
wrists wide open

corkscrew
wine
red

another bottle in my hand
not like life
not like women
not like
one chance is all you ever get

8

slap me with your promiscuity
tell me that you just don't care
hit me with all of your
passionate dispassion
me too, me too

give me a whore/hand me a slut
gutter tramps like I
who walk the night

that is were life is lived
where the truth is known

       leave India for the holy
       Israel for the fool
       I'll take southeast asia
       where it just doesn't matter anymore

         I'm tired of chasing
         that vestal virgin dream

9

sitting staring out of bamboo shades
bamboo shades
lead to the a summers' day

      bamboo shades/prison bars
           life in the big city

watching a movie on T.V.
isolation
a glass of wine, red
isolation

      the unit of isolation
      easy unity
      passive submission
      a saved life
      in an elementary vision
      bound from the world
      saved from the dis-ease

      but desire it still hides
      in every corner
      and personally
      I prefer the chance

      moments
           in the life of an unwilling recluse

10

sip the grape
it has become
so un-fashionable/so uncool
sip the grape
while american society
the mindless masses
follow all the trends
listen to all the lies

sip the grape
drink down a moment of illusion
in a life that passes by
all too fast

11

night time
>> all the time

sometimes I would just prefer to
>> go to bed

women, or alone
always running
a need to run
somewhere/nowhere
like jogging on a tread mill
like tires in the sand
like ice in the sunshine
or a greased female body next to mine

to bed
but three is poetry to write
literature to create
and you know
that I am years behind
all the going to nowhere
the cuming, not the becoming

nighttime, all the time
and the chase after
that oh so allusive
reason for the literature
reason for the poetry
female form
of a feminine dream

12

a park
surrounded by a city
I listen to the hum
it can be heard from all around
from all directions
shattering
the almost silence
breaking it w/ an almost sound

someone's hard earned day
ticks on/ticks by
I spend it
like the dollars and cents
of the moving world
conquering all
accomplishing nothing

me, I would prefer to listen
to the almost silence
to the constant sound
feel the perfection
of the imperfection
of life that ticks on and on

13

I am surround by time
ticking by
    and you know
    that there isn't a thing I can do about it

        I went out on my patio this evening
        a patio that overlooks the sea
        I watched the sunset
        but it was gone
        before it could be grasped

and I guess
that it would not be so bad
but I feel like I have so much bullshit
so much other bullshit
that I should be doing
that is, other than
spending credit card money
that I don't have
making love to a chick
that I don't dig
and running somewhere to nowhere
    across the off reaches of the globe

but then what is art
I guess it is feeling good
doing what you are doing
but what about
when you are an artist
feeling bad
about what you are not doing

    so tick-tock
        fuck the clock

14

a dream just too tired to be lived
too tired to be known

with the pounding/hyperventilating
heart attack
of the known world
pounding down
on my soul
there is so little room
left for vision

so jump start
the life start
back to where it all began

       fall down
       one too many times
       there is no one to give
       the dreamer a hand

       left to their own devise
       of the self demise

a drink = a dream
a kiss = a moment

but nothing always = nothing

15

hospital walls
gray, white, light green, faded blue
into her room
she lay on the bed
it almost looks high tech
almost fashion-passion
like the style which she embraced

chrome metal
risen steel boundaries
holding her in
like the bars of a prison
the sweet bird in a cage

and plastic tubes
they form the veins
which led into her arm

as her skin
blended into the aloneness
of the white hospital sheets

who else has known them
who else has been trapped
by their grasp

      yes, you are dying
      please go to a better place
      a place, where you will be happy
      go to somewhere where the living
      does not make you sad

      and you will live in my heart
          forever

forever and ever and ever
until someday when I join you
where life is not so hard
and the dreams do not crumble
like so many crumbs in our hands

I love you, good bye

16

lay on the couch
all day long
damned, if I know what to run

T.V. on
pre-wash the brain-wash
"why? does your brain need washing?"

      glass of wine
      in my hand
      a bottle or three
      over there

      a babe
      or two
      across the city
            they are just not worth the drive

so $0 = 0$
nothing all the same
let me lay here
doing the nothing

      nothing
            the purest form of art

a world that is going someplace
a world that is going by
a million millionaires
a billion wanta be/will be/could be
talking of their finances
speaking of the cars they drive

me
I prefer to refer
to dreaming visions

me
I would rather not live
than to live the lie

17

love poetry on a napkin
and the days that do not mean
anything at all

> the L.A. sun is pouncing
> pounding hard
> on the plexiglas patio
> on which I sit

> people eat
>   all around me

> discussion life
>   politics
>   boxing
>   and karma

> as the stylish cars
> motor down wilshire boulevard
>   they cruise right on by me

> and me
> I sit here
> discussing the silence
> living the dream
> for whatever it is worth

> and I write of a love
> that I ran away from today
> yes, it was just this morning
> after we made love last night
> 4:32 AM
> I know because I looked at the clock

but rich babes now poor
all they want to do is complain
insult the dreams of a dreamer
remind you
of all that you are not

but all is nothing anyway
and you can see how fast it goes away
rich babes now poor
their eyes promise a life of disaster

I walked out
with an ounce of pride
which sure beats living through
a hell of dispassion

and so
here I sit
awaiting breakfast
11:28 A.M.
bombay burger
as the sun pours onto the plexiglas
creating kill humidity
reminding me of bombay

      making me feel/making me wish
      that I was back there
      in india again

18

java/the grape
stay awake/alter the state
poetry to write
paintings to bring into existence

like new souls being born
rhythms being composed
a reason/a purpose
late night/all night
leave the days for the working
the saints of this world
the night
it is for the dreamers

> a drink from a cup
> a sip from a glass
> like poison/like passion
> like passages
> a key to this night

slice me another cup of the java
stay up all night long
a glass of the grape
to take the edge off
while I live the dream
here
where nothing really matters
where I melt into the alones of art
exist in the nothing worth living for
and dream
oh yes
I do have a few dreams

19

3:00 A.M.
and another drink
for another reason
god
I am going to be sick tomorrow

throw a frozen pizza
into the over
and it just doesn't mean
anything at all

like the drink
like the money
like the babe
I made love to tonight

there she is
over there
passed out in my bed

the nothing of conquest
the lust of momentary love

a moment lived
only for the poetry
the price
it is always paid later

20

and the night
it goes down hard
but it better than sitting at home
being married/getting old

       w/ every dance
           there is another chance

so morning
well, afternoon is here
out of bed
time to lick my wounds
move from the bed
to the couch
my dick
still a bit twisted
too much sex
too much cocaine
evening last
my stomach
none too pretty
a bit too much of the drink

but a moment to dream
a life to steal
and it all mean nothing
anyway

fuck the holy
they know nothing
leave the living
for the dreamers
who have experienced
it all

21

I am strutting my bad self
in this khaki style clothing store
when up comes this babe
rap'n to her friend
in the *nehongo*
(japanese)

yeah, she was fine
move on/move in
strut in/strut out

finally
she and her child bearing/child carrying friend
were separate
apart
I move on over
give her a sweet little word
a speech/a saying
in her native tongue

we spoke of tokyo
we spoke of L.A.

age and names

and then up comes here friend
if looks could kill...

so back up/back off
went and paid for the clothing
w/ plastic passion
money that I do not have

she came up to pay after me
I said, "see you later. someplace/some dream,"
I spoke to her in japanese

I walked out the door
in all my empty and alone glory
and style

      another one of those dreams
      that just begged to happen
      another one of those times
      when I should have done this
            could have done that

      a moment of life
      cast, only to this poetry
      and the *never-never-land*
      of what might have been

22

the night hits hard
lost in the confusion
of this lost life
I drive down the boulevard
me, in my 1964 porsche

I could stop/I should go home
but fuck it
I drive on
into the abyss of nowhere
        supremely fast

the world cries out to me
to pay my bills
the passion screams to me
to spend money I do not have

my bad little '64 of a 356 sc
it was suggest
that I sell it
sell it, to pay the rent

now, I guess I am a few years older than it
six
if I count them on the dial
and no-one/no-thing
last forever

        so, I look to the rear view mirror
        look at my face
        look into my own eyes
        and sell it/ sell me
        no thank you
        I think it is time

for both of us
to roll up shop
and die

drive somewhere/no-where
like, you know, driving along
and put the pedal to the metal
punch it real hard
feel the g-force pull me back
and guide us into *never-never-land*
where the rent is free
no break down/no bills to pay
and it's gotta feel better

a whole lot than this

Chapter 3

No Kisses for the Sinner

It is perhaps sad that one may only see things through their own perception -- though they may try and claim to do otherwise.

It is also sad that though one may believe another to have the ability to be something other than what they are -- what they are is simply that, what they are.

This is the story and the case of her, and the sad truth being, what I believed she could become, was, in fact, not what she was. We both paid the price.

1

the sun bleeds
its warm presence unto me as I lay dying
stabbed in the heart
like some drunken warrior
confounded by purpose
confused by reason
while illusion dances upon my soul

>and the sun bleeds its purpose unto me
>whispering it reluctance of coming forth
>to break the spell the spell
>of a relentless night

2

and in the ending passion
of an ending night
of an ending love
ending so fast /ending so soon

oh it is so true

and the situations surround me
no where to run
desire in its purest form
wished for

       she says she wished for me

prayed for

       I have been asked for before

and it closes in
no place to run
no way out
my car is trapped
blocked by another ride
behind it
so unfair
I can not move

and she, she sings
"hey now, hey now."

and she, she asks me,
"would you like to be in a relationship with me?"

and here I am
here I sit
go/stay?
no way to know

and all the passion
is lust in visions
of what never is

I suppose
I wished
I prayed
for her as well
but it all seems so strange
my dreams/my desires
so unanswered
and yet, here they are

answered in such a way

but like I have long said,
"any dream will do."
well any dream it is
any dream/any reason
but...
just but...
its touch
its vision could have been
so much sweeter
its touch
so much more pure

3

ah, the midnight hour has come
it whispers of its passion
it whispers of the mystic wind
so, good night
and remember
remember everything

4

in the love
the love that loves me now
never is there a space
a space so pure
so pure it hurts

they promise you everything
       everything
       everything
       everything
             it sounds so poetic

    so poetic
    so much of nothing
    they promise you love
    so much love it will hurt

    but in reality, it hurts to think of
    being in love with her

    but my heart pounds
    my head spins
    and I have no place left to run
    no where at all

as my current love lies next to me
asleep

asleep in *never-never-land*
la-la-land
6:00 A.M.
she sleeps
I should go to sleep
and move onto another/a different dream

75

5

I saw a picture of her
a picture sitting upon a living room table

> slightly out of focus
> the colors faded into the sunlight
> but her form
> was placed into infinity
> her look
> her glance
> the image of the goddess
>
> the image of the goddess
> but not the one
> which I have come to know

her photograph
faded by the light
faded by the focus
distant
hazy
a forgotten goddess
she has forgotten it herself
leaving her body to be used
her mind to be stolen
and when that was all completed
she handed herself to me
to me
too late
nothing could be repaired

6

I woke
to her asian eyes this morning
early morning
her time
not mine

I woke
to her asian eyes
and they were not covered
with the make-up
I had seen the night before

I woke and her face
it was not painted with the colors
I have come to expect

her eyes
they were simple
no longer
were they scared
from the years
of gaining
external wisdom
by and for external thought

        yes, they were almost free
                yes, they were almost new

I woke
to her asian eyes this morning
and they glowed the radiance
of ancient purity/ancient thought
the promise of poetry
which I had never seen in them before

7

she asks,
"why don't you ever want to go out and be social?"

"sorry babe, I'm not a social guy."

she says,
"why don't you want to meet my friends?"

"because we have nothing in common."

"but they think I am making all this up.
        they think I am making you up."

"you are."

8

force feed me a cup of illusion
yes, I do need a dream
a dream
any dream
yes, any dream will do

force feed me a cup of illusion
in the dim light
of her asian eyes

force feed me
please

force feed me a cup of salvation

or must I run away
run to where the visions are pure
run to where there is sweet freedom
run to where there are no walls
and illusions come true

force feed me a cup of forgiveness
for yes, I have sinned
I have looked
I have seen
I have taken a hold of a dream
a dream in the dream of
where any dream will do

I have held it
I have taken it
I have known it
I did so as I saw that
it was not what I wanted

not what I needed
not what I thought it would be at all

I took it
I held it
I knew its forms was imperfect
yet, I took it anyway

force feed me a cup of salvation
for yes, I have sinned
I believed any dream will do
well, any dream is what I got
and it was unworthy
still the same

9

her blood drips upon me
she softly rubs it in

spread your love disease upon me
spread it
make sure that there can be no escape

once it seemed to matter
now it all appears too late
      loss and gain
      all the same
      I can never escape

she raises her body
her blood drips upon me
she moves slowly
applying it softly

spread your love disease
leave me
no escape

10

I woke up in the morning
my morning
12:00 P.M., or so
I made my way into the bathroom
for the traditional
shower and shave

as I stand there
thinking of the night before
of the woman
who had been in my arms
as I stand there thinking
of a million reasons
to leave her alone
a million ways
to get her to do the same
I look down
and there upon my shoulder
intertwined with my long blond hair
was a long straight black hair
one of hers
from the night before

she gets up 7:30 A.M.
work, she has to be to
I am left alone
to the mystical breakfast
on the shore
and the memories
of the night(s) before

but there is so much more to life
so much more to love
than reasons

beyond no good reason
and lasting embraces
in the night

11

can it be
that the forgiveness
lies in the arms of a stranger
a stranger who is known by many

      can it be known
      can it be held
      can I find
      can I feel it anywhere at all

I thought that it may be found
in her arms/in her kiss

      her kiss
      I have known it
      as many other before
      she can not remember the number
      lost count
      in lost time
      and more than one is one too many for me

      but me too
      long ago I lost count
      so who am I to judge

once the secret it is lost
once the secret is known
and than there is nothing left to prove

with nothing left to know
nothing left to prove
knowledge loses all its meaning

teach me what I have never known

12

she lives
just above the sunset strip
just up the street from *the whiskey a-go-go*

a dream of the clothed in leather
a dream for those who
worship the illusions of the night

I lived it
that dream
but that dream was so long ago

       lived it/had it
       it gave me no reason

but there she sits
her apartment on the hill
believing that her location
makes her who she is
makes her more
something
less than nothing

but when you live
in the noise
the crowds
next to the polluted want-a-bes
all you embrace is their pollution

not the true wisdom
of the night

13

the love of illusion
yes, the love of delusion
and how it comes down so hard
so hard on me
so hard on what is
and what is longed for
or better said, what isn't

isn't, isn't

and it has been had
so many times before
before, where all the dead dreams lie

tomorrow, where all the fantasies live

live in their immaterialness
live, but are not real
yet, they live just the same

14

life in the mainstream
alive but so unreal
real is here
but it feels so unreal
so much less
than it could have been

you are breathing
your mainstream onto me
you make me feel false
unreal/untrue

but here is where we are
and this is what we have to deal with

what is this?
what it is,
isn't it?

in all its perfection

15

the kiss
it is oh so alluring
the lie
so allusive
but let us lay down here
lay down
and hold one another
and pretend
that before never existed

16

confusion
this dance goes on and on
will it ever stop/can it ever stop

choose love
as it stares at me
the past
will it ever be gone /can it ever be gone

gone today
gone tomorrow
gone forever
forever and ever

if it is gone than why does it haunt me so

kiss me
one more time
convince me
to stay with you another day
convince me
try to make me believe
convince me
I want to believe
convince me
of my confusion

17

she telephones me
she says,
"yes, I will quite my job.
      and you will do something flaky.
      like leave me again.
      I know it, I just know it."

"your instincts
      they serve you well," I answer.

"But make a choice
      a chance
      for a dream
      as momentary as that dream may be
      a chance
      to live
      to feel
      to do nothing
      to accomplish nothing
      the essence of life
      so make a choice."

18

now it is not
that she is not a serious babe
and it is not
that she doesn't know how to dress
it is just
that she never wants
to take walks by the ocean
feel the wind blow
in the mountain air
it is just that she prefers
new york city
over san francisco
and she just does not know how
to do nothing
nothing at all

now it is not
that I do not love her
as far as love may go
and it is not
that I would not want to hold her forever
it is just that she does not know how to dream

      to dream
      the answer of the ancients
      the key to the mysteries
      the love of the love for the love
      like the wind
      you never see it
      but you can feel that it is there

19

I almost wish
that I could marry her
I almost wish
that I loved her more
I almost wish
I had never lied to her
I almost wish
a lot of things

but things
they never seem to end
and the world
well, it goes on and on

      the world goes on
      time ticks on
      life moves on
      and love
      well, it fades

but in all the realms
of *never-never-land*
the land that surrounds all time
all is
what ever it is
and what never was
will always be
I can not erase it
though I have tried

      love lost
      love that kills
      point the gun at me
      and fire at will

20

I look to my side
there lays a black hair
a black hair
from the woman
the woman I made love to this evening

and though I can never love her again
I will let the black hair rest

rest in its place
I will let it
sleep next to me tonight

       one more night
       for the memories
       one more night
       for the dreams
       one more night
       for no reason at all
       one more night
       for the screams

21

she asked me
are we the same as you two were
am I the same as she
did our needs bring us together
like your needs led you to her

no, it is not need
that brought us together
desire is a far better word
desire and need
are so far apart
like desire has made me
walk away from you

now, I am not saying
we were not in love
and I am not saying
it did not feel good
but desire
no, it is not need
and desire
it always seems to die
when the illusion wears off

22

and the kisses
embrace the day
the touch
embraces the night
and when all are interweaved
all are intertwined
the truth
it be spoken
the truth
be spoken to the few

and therefore
and thereof
the lies
they no longer matter
the actions
they no longer care
and the love
it is spread
deeply in the night
lasting until the day

than the day
speaks its goodbyes

23

the kisses are for those
who eat the late night pies
the dreams are for those
that live
the love is for those
who are believers
and tonight
is for those of us
who never look back

> is there ever a kiss misplaced
> a love longed for
> more than lust
> a feeling embraced
> than turned away
> a night
> that just goes on too long

> every dream has its price
> for life is filled with lies

> every love
> has a destiny to end
> life is simply too short a time

and when there is no more use
in pretending
and when there is
no more reasons why

a kiss becomes just a kiss
a dream just a dream
and then
mysticism fills the air

24

the kiss
it looks so sweet
but it feels so deadly
attraction/distraction
I've lived on the outskirts of hell

gray, it is not so clean
not so shiny
or is it simply dirty white

gray is the color of the city
I have slept on the outskirts of hell

there is no place to run to
no place left to hide
it all is the same
one moment flowing to the next
one feeling into the other
the next to the other
I have been embraced by the outskirts of hell

25

her words,
they speak to me,
she says,

> "well, at least I have lived.
> you know, I could write a book.
> a book, just like you write.
> what would you have rather I had been,
> a nice little girl
> growing up like those around me?"

> "maybe, yes maybe."

living it is for fools
fools who believe the lie
the lie
of supply and demand
conquest and conquer
fools, who never will see
that all the living
adds up to nothing

> maybe we should sit
> and watch
> maybe it would be better
> that way
> simply let the world go by
> in its time
> and believe
> that gain and experience
> mean nothing at all

> maybe
> I do not know

for there are mystics
who danced upon the path
who walk on both sides
of the wall
mystics like me who live
mystics like me who dream

believing that every take down
is a lift up
every lie
is eventual truth

so maybe
I do not know

but both sides of the wall
it is a difficult way
difficult and distant
in all the realms of mind
back and forth
going nowhere
going everywhere
where, is no place at all

so maybe
just maybe
it is truth
not to give in
truth
to run away
truth
to sit and watch
as the water settles to mud
and the truth
to merges with I do not care

it is not easy
that I know
for the world
hands its hooks
into everyone

easy or hard
one leads to the other
the different to the same

day to night
night to day

      maybe, yes maybe

26

I almost believed
that we were meant to be
yes, I almost believed
that we could be
could be forever

       forever and ever and ever
       yes, I almost believed
       that we were butter
       melting into each other

yes
and when I look into your eyes
when I don't look too deep
and when I try not to see

       see who you were
       see what you were
       yes, I almost believe
       that I could love you forever
       forever and ever and ever

and when the wheel spins around
and the truth comes down
it is like a knife
in my heart
tearing me apart
because I almost believed
that you and I
could have been forever
forever and ever and ever

so I try to tell myself
do not open your eyes

keep them closed
and just compromise
never look to far
never look to deep
but the truth comes down
and the messages they speak
but I almost believed
that it was a dream
yes, I almost believed
that you were forever
forever and ever and ever

27

I called her
on the telephone
spoke to her
on the telephone line
it meant nothing
not anything at all

     zero in a zero world

     now I could go
     to her place tonight
     for you know that
     I do have the keys
     I could go there
     for I know that
     she waits for me
     I could go there
     and make nothing
     equal even less

     do you love me
     she asks

     I hang up

now the games and dance go on and on
and I've got no more time

     no more time
     for my lies
     to mean nothing

     but than nothing
     does not mean anything at all

I always initiate the first blow
strike hard
is the rule of the game
never let your opponent move first
always keep the advantage clear

if the opponent connects
if their blow hits home
strike back hard
devastate them
take no prisoners
none at all

love and lust
and relationships
they are all for the fool
play them
play them well
I do

I called her on the telephone line
there is no reason why
I call the game
call it to win it
one more time
I push the drama
push it to one more scene

     everything is
     as everything isn't
     and there is no reason why
     good night/goodbye
     she wants me
     she wants the game
     she wants the lies

that I have told her
she wants the fantasy

but love is love
only by definition

definitions
they always seem to change

let them change
as change will change
like the wind
in the california winter sky

the last words that I spoke to her
a hang up
to her question

        it said, yes
        yes, I do
        let me come to you
        please heal all of my pain

but nothing ever equals anything
zero is still the same
the same
it never seems to stay that way
        the same
a hang up on the telephone line

28

did I tell you
that I lied
when I told
that I loved you

      no reason
      is the best reason
      of all

I lied
when I told you
that I loved you
I lied to you
I lied to myself

you had what it took to get me
you did not have what it took to keep me
keep me with you

      and the passion of existence
      and the prospect of forever
      it never has the ability to last
      so when the kisses come in
      and the dreams die young
      the flowers that may bloom tomorrow
      have all that it takes
      to give birth to a new dream

29

she cried to me on the telephone
a pay phone on melrose
she cried
for my love
cried, like I have cried for love

      for love
      love that she wants
      she cried
      for me to be with her
      I wish I could
      she cried
      I will cry
      but I can not allow myself to
      not now
      not until I am alone
      when my tears will not be heard
      by her,
       my west hollywood chinese princess
      at a pay phone on melrose
      alone...

30

a collect call
comes on the telephone lines
why is it
that the babe's always call me collect

     a collect call comes in
          a collect call goes on

"do you want me to come over?"
"why," I ask
"because you love me."
"I do?"

but than the subject changes
     she tells me
     that she would be slapping me
     if I were standing next to her

"a lot of *cha-cha's* going by," she says
"what's a *cha-cha?"* I ask
"you know,
     the kind of girl you always fall in love with.
     that kind of girl that you always want to
     leave.
     you know, *cha-cha's,*
     party girls,
     chinese party, girls,
     like I used to be."

I guess she knows me well
and I guess it is true
that if I had been there
she would have slapped me
for checking out the scene

but isn't what you once were
the foundation
the formation
of what you are

she and I
her mind
my lies
it never did add up to two
so with her dollars in tow
her mind on me
with her finger
on the push buttons
I get a collect telephone call.

"do you want me to come over?"
"why?"

31

I wish all the hours of time
spent talking to her
on the telephone line
could equal its weight in creativity
equal its weight in gold

the words that are spoken
tears and fears
love and lies
dreaming
as we both tend to do

I wish when all was said
and when all was done
it could mean more
than simple foolish emotions
simple foolish sounds

than all would be
of so much more validity

creativity
turned to gold

32

she sends me flowers
she sends them to my door
she sends me roses
roses by the dozen

with each arrival
there comes a card

I love you

I love you forever

forever
forever

today they arrived
the flowers, in the evening
the flowers, of the evening
they came with a card
a card that said

still dreaming…

well, dream on my asian sweetheart
dream
all that you can dream
dream
forever and ever
dream
that you will be with me again

for maybe if you dream
dream just hard enough
maybe if you dream

dream with enough intensity
maybe if you dream
forever and ever
than you may see me again

for whenever the vision has faded
whenever the truth comes out
and whenever there is just too much known
and not enough felt
there is one reason left
a reason to walk away

so send me flowers
if you have the inclination
I will receive them in style
send me roses
if you have the money
but you did not lay them at my feet

        so kiss tomorrow
        as it embraces you
        kiss it
        as you have kissed me
        kiss it hello
        as I kiss you goodbye

        goodbye
        forever and ever

33

I could not help but fell the distance
the distance
as I glanced into your eyes

as love dances
as love always seems to do
it has separated
separated her and I

reached the point of flux
where her world
can not meet mine
mine can not see hers

so the movement
it is in motion
the lessening of the love
it has begun

she will chase
I will run
but in the end
it will be the same
it will be gone

34

her body
it has lost all of its illusion
no longer
do I long
to embrace within her arms
intimacy has not replaced the boredom
love has never grown
in the place that infatuation once held

there seems only one answer
the answer
it can only remain the same

as in all those in front of me
and all those before
the answer is to walk away

now I wish it could have been more silent
silent parting
the ultimate art
but it grew loud
made itself notices

      loud
      it made itself heard

with all that is lost
and with all that is gained
and all that is once loved
than no longer loved
there seems to be a rhythm
seems to be a familiarity
seems to be a sign
they all seem so much alike

but it describes only
the same pain

her body
it has lost all of its illusion
no longer
do I long
to embrace within its arms
intimacy has not replaced the boredom
love has never grown
in the place that infatuation once held

35

some women you can not love
some women you do not want to love
some women you pretend to love
some women you almost love
and some women
the more you love them
the more it hurts
so all you can do is run away

me, I run very well

36

a rose pedal
lays on the floor
on the floor
under a chair
a neo-modern
nuevo-high tech chair
a chair
I purchased at a thrift store
$10.00

the rose pedal lay there
from a dozen roses
given to me by a girl
a girl which I tried to love
I tired hard

oh, she was so beautiful
dressed in her west hollywood
glam-slam style

      eyes, they were so asian
      lips, they were painted so red
      hair, it was so black
      love, it could have been

yes, it is true
for I was fooled by a pretty face

a pretty face
like the roses

the roses they were red
yet they faded
they died

they fell apart
one of the pedals
now lay upon my floor

        red
        dark red
        like her painted lips

her lips
they would caress me
they would paint my body
leave their imprint
upon my soul

        lips
        red
        imprint
        like it has left on my life

the rose pedal
lay on my floor
under my neo-modern
nuevo-high tech chair
from the thrift store

the pedal red
it reminds me
of the roses
which she gave me

the pedal
it reminds me
of a woman
which I tried to love
I tried very hard
it is true

118

I was fooled
by a beautiful face

the rose pedal
it is no longer alive
dead like our love
the little of it that there was

gone
faded
fading like the memory
of a west hollywood
glam-slam chinese girl
who seduced me
tried to make me love her
promised me everything
but it did not work

it all lay in its decomposingness

our love
the memory
just like
the rose pedal
which lay upon my floor

37

she cries on the telephone
I have heard her tears before
she cries
I ask her
to please calm down
but I hear the tears ringing
as they stab
a tender spot in my soul

she cries on the telephone
I have heard these tears before
I tell her
I will come over
try to make her feel better
she wants to know why
for I can not promise her tomorrow

all my words of forever
turned into being nothing but lies
she is right
I am wrong
I have failed
by not being able
to love her fully
not being able to
but promising her that I could

she cries on the telephone
I have heard these tears before
I have made her cry too many times

38

what do you do
when your dream dies
or a least the closest thing to it
so far/thus far

blood red lips
asian eyes
a girl
from glam-slam
west hollywood

I have painted her
a thousand times

what do you do
when what was
is washed away
wiped clean
by your own hands
put to rest
by your own deeds

is it
what was there
or was it
what was lacking
that made me continue
to stay
continue to run away

was it
or is it
they forever
leave a blank answer

in my mind

and yes, I remember the dream
and yes, I remember the dare
and yes, I remember desire
to find someone just like her

and yes, I know the longing
and yes, I the pain

the desire to have
to hold
and than let go
only to desire again

so closes another chapter
of my life

no longer can it be said
that it is still an open book
with pages remaining to be read

what do you do
when you run so hard from someone
and when you stop
and look around
and find yourself
all alone

and what do you do
when the near perfect dream dies

39

she tells me
that she forgets
forgets what it is like to sleep with me
I tell her
remember
remember forever and ever
for that is all that you now have now
       the memories

and love gets old
and she gets angry
angry
that I do not
fall at her hallowed feet

and love dies
where it was never born
gone
forever more

40

and when my eyes are closed
it is magic/pure magic

the magic it has increased with time

and when we are together
together and in each others arms
if I don't think to hard
I never want to be in another's

love it is not for strangers
love it is only for the fool
love, if only it were the only thing
but all the world goes on and on

and when you cry
I cry
when you feel lost
I am lost
and when you have those feeling
of not wanting to go on
they are no different
than the ones I have come to know

but my eyes, it seems
they can not stay closed
my dreams
through the years
have become quite defined
and if love were enough
to heal all the wounds
than the love which you have given me
would cure all my pain

you have touched me
like no one before
that is why I write this verse
you have given me gifts
which no one in the past
ever took the time to give
that is why I wish
it were all so different

and if it were only the love
than the only love
you would be
but haunting obsessing memories
they continue to follow us
close on our trail
from a world of yours
of which I want no part

kiss me my love
the girl I wished for
and I will kiss you
a kiss from the man
you dreamed of
        a kiss it will be
        a kiss forever more
        a kiss goodbye

yes, I have grown to love
love as much
as most before
but a kiss
it will be
a kiss goodbye
for my eyes can not remain closed

and the magic
though it is strong
does not have the strength
to make them stay that way

but when my eyes are not open
it is such magic
magic as I have never known before
it is the magic
that I will remember
remember as I think of you
remember
that when my eyes were closed
I loved you
like no one before

41

hours of time/telephone lines
her words they say nothing to me
hours of time/talking with no mind
the words of a fool

lie
though she doesn't know she lies
but the words they equal un-truths
just the same/all in the game
the dance
that goes on and on

promise me love
she says to me
promise me time
her words cry
promise me forever
forever and ever
promise me until death do us part

promise me

words they go so far
so far into *never-never-land*

words they equal zero
zero
the figure that describes
life and its emptiness

the hours they tick by
time misspent
time I can never get it back

but her screams to the night
the wail of her tears
the promises that she makes
and the lies
and her fears

never, never, never

so let me write these words
to compensate for her tears
let me write these words
to make something
of all the time that has been spent
all the time that has been lost

written words
her promises
and the telephone line

hours of time/telephone lines
her words they say nothing to me

hours of time/telephone lines
talking with no mind
the words of a fool

42

I suppose that I am sorry
that I have made you cry
I suppose that I am sorry
that I have brought tears to your eyes
I suppose
that is the case
but the truth being told
and the lies being known
it is
what has happened

and if I had been wise
if I had not been such a fool
if I had the strength
to walk away clean
than perhaps your tears
may never had needed to fall

but I was a dreamer
a dreamer
in search of a dream
        a dreamer
        speaking what a dreamer does
        saying that any dream will do

well, you were that
that, anyway
a dream
that lived on
to be my nightmare
a dream
from which I had to run

but when there is no way out
there is certainly no way in
and never
sounds so much better
than forever
so the kiss goodbye
it felt so sweet
yet, it had to be dealt
in a bitter broth

so tomorrow show signs
of a new a different dream
today's sound
rings in my ears
with the tears you have cried
with the lies we have lied
and never
sounds so much better
than forever
and no longer will any dream do

I suppose that I am sorry
that I have made you cry
I suppose that I am sorry
that I have brought tears
to your eyes

43

she tells me on the telephone,
"the last thing I will ever have from you
      is a note that says, fuck you."

I told her,
"I will send you some poetry."
those were the final words that I spoke to her
I hung up

      well here it is
      and here they are

      poetry
      words

      to a woman...
      who was not too much of anything
      except a waste of my time
      and a reason to write

and the dreams
they call us out
the desires
they make us fall
and the screams
they go on forever
forever and ever and ever

and she could never be
what I wanted her to be
never could the past be erased
and I could never agree to be
all that she wanted of me

I could not be
the dream which she called for

so I left a note
fuck you
and I walked away

a night/a day
they all moved together
it was only a moment ago

now time goes on
as it tends to do
dreams fade/desires change
and clarity becomes all the same

      and when the moment
      where any dream will do
      fades slowly
      into the place
      where only a specific
      desire will be true
      than life ticks on
      I move on
      and the only truth
      is the closing words
      I wrote to her
      fuck you

44

yes, that is her
the one with the bright red lip stick
and the sunglasses on
yes, she was mine
yes, she could have been mine forever
but it was I
who walked away

yes, that is her
the one with the jet black hair
the black leather jacket
and the chinese eyes hidden
yes, she was mine

mine for a moment
a moment in time

yes, she flowed away
flowed away
to the halls of the illusion
where all the tainted goddesses dwell

yes, she flowed
and I have never seen her again

45

is it I
who buys the ticket
to be alone
is it I?

is it I
who makes other's choices
makes other's minds
is it I?

is it I
who can't erase
what has long ago happened
can I pretend
that it never did exist
is it I?

is it I
who is lost in the masses
lost in the form
formless as it may be
is it I?

is it I
who spins in the whirlpool
spins in the hurricane
and can not find a way out
is it I?

is it I
who longs to dream
longs to love
longs to long
is it I?

is it I
who chooses to be alone
is it I?

no, I don't think so
no

Chapter 4

Last Will and Testament
According to the Divine Rites of the Drug Cocaine

Sometimes the world pounds down hard on you and illusion offers a far better alternative to the hell granted by the mundane/by the alone. You move out into that promised land but perhaps you will never return.

If drugs are so bad, then why do they make you feel so good? So good until you take that one step out over the edge, where your grasp on reality is shaky and your ability to remain alive is completely removed from your control. That is what this text is about: that desire of illusion, that one step out over the edge; that place where experience is gained, realizations are had, enlightenment is known, and death may inadvertently become your only friend.

1

almost forgot about my tape recorder
twelfth of June
just about 1:31 A.M.

I might die tonight
I am, I am fucking way too high
I did way too much coke but...
if I do go
I want no one to cry any tears over me
because then I will be free

I have a certain remorse
about my lack of accomplishment
musically, literarily, artistically
but, I hope no one cries any tears over me

I am walking on the pier right now
I am going to talk in a few minutes if I make it

(my breath is shallow)

walking down pier avenue, now
past the bars
trying to grasp onto a bit of reality
my heart is like, is like
hurts weird

people coming so...

hermosa avenue now
turning to just walk down by the bars
then I'll go back down to *the strand*

oh, my heart hurts

and I am fighting for air

for awhile when I...
the reason I keep stopping
is my mouth is so dry
it's funny there was a soda machine
but I didn't have any change

I keep licking my lips
but ...
I keep feeling like I am going to pass out
and now I'm feeling like
I'm going to do it again

funny, in my observation notebook
I kept writing
a whole bunch of observations
about a cocaine high
and this is the one place not to get to
where you're going to die
and I...
if I have a heart attack...
what have you...

(cough)

I initially thought to return home
just after about a block of walking
on *the strand*

(deep exhale)

hard to breathe

because I wanted to ditch my coke in...
If I went down

that way I wouldn't/couldn't
get arrested for at least that...

because I have a lot of coke at home

so I don't know if walking is good for me
I think it is
it kind of keeps my system working, you know
but talking and walking
it is hard for me to concentrate...
on breathing, and so...

    (laughter)

I have never been this high
actually my feeling is pretty gro-o-o-o

    (end of side of tape)

had to turn the tape over

    (deep exhale)

actually my feeling,
as I was saying, is pretty grounded
but my body is breaking down

    (deep exhale)

so I'm going to stop talking now
and concentrate on breathing
I don't know whether it's a good idea
to go home and take a valium or not
could be though
could be

I'll have to think

     (burp)

cocaine burp
and I've been drinking all this java tonight
funny, I wanted to...

trying to get some liquid to swallow
nada there

nada
nada
nada

but it's funny
I wanted to like
start pushing myself to start
staying up later again
four or five in the A.M.
so I could get creative
and start working on the books
in the night
like I like to do

     I've been fighting the remaining
     last journey to asia
     jetlag

so I drank some steamed *espresso*
two giant cups of it
and that stuff usually puts me up,
you know, till the early morning hours
one cup usually does
but because of my...
still not complete adjustment

to the time zone...

there are some people though...
OK
kinda past
what was I saying
awh, about the coffee, you know, and the time
zone
so I wanted to start staying up later
and getting creative
to alleviate my artistic frustration but...

may have done one notch too many

interestingly enough what I did
see what I did
what I did was bang down
two very heavy lines
just before I left
because I had come down,
you know, to a reasonable level
and awh...
then I had to have that typical cocaine
go back and do one more thAng
that one more line

so I went and dug my stuff out
where I stash it
in the drawer
and chopped up
another couple lines

and I banged 'em
they were heavy back up lines

and I think that...

you know...
because I was down
but I'm still very high
I've been snorting coke all night
        all day and all night

but I didn't have the high feeling

        (deep exhale)

and so awh...
that's what did it
is that, that awh,
last minute quarter gram
that I put up my nose

probably did down about a gram-ski tonight
maybe more
maybe plus
maybe gram-ski plus

funny, here comes a bicycle rider
so I'm going to chill for a second

cocaine comes on

he just rode by but...

cocaine, you know it's that
that waiting for the high
but then when it hits
it's a BAP!

but you know the feeling is
is that lying promise

I will never do this again
if I live through it

but awh...
you know, it's interesting observations
I really don't have an addictive desire to this
drug
but it's more like an experiential type thing
it's like
why not go ahead and do it
you know, get that kind of head
and get the distance to where...
if I don't create
I don't hate myself

        (deep exhale)

etc.
let's see what it does

I get periodic dizzy spells
I'm walking here...

so I guess I said all there is to say, awh

I believe I'll make it
and I believe I'll do cocaine again
but I should set down, seeeet doooown
some kind of definition to myself
because I'm not the young man I once was
you know
although, I'm not old,
I guess twenty-nine, coming up fast on thirty
but um...
my heart is not that great

        (deep exhale)

it has always given me bits of problems
here and…

I feel real dizzy right now
I feel really high

there's somebody up there, but um…

I, I hope the walking has helped me
I think it must for it gets my system circulating

then I got to go home and drink some…
water
a lot of it
no more *java* though, not this evening

but if I live through this
the experience will be well worth it
and as I'm saying
I'll probably do it again
but hopefully with someone else this time
because, you know…
this is just no good alone
to get in this position where nobody's there
to dump your coke for you
to keep you from the arm's of the law
and take you to the hospital
if you need to go

I think it's really bad
there's somebody out on their patio
I think they just walked in

it's almost summer

148

although it's cool tonight

a lot of people out in the late night

it's now...
about 1:41 A.M.

god, it seems a lot longer than just ten minutes
when I said it was, 1:31

god, I almost went out/passed out
I got to, to grab reality
I can't let myself slip

      (deep exhale)

god, I'm really wa... way wasted
my head is spinning right now
I can't let myself go down

it was worse though
when I first started out
well, no
I think this is about
this is about equal

it's the talking
I should breathe better

I'm going to leave the tape on just in case
I go down,
but ... as I say
if I die
then I'll be free

don't cry no tears over me

(deep gasp)

(steps, steps, steps)

(deep gasp, for air)

this is about as worse as it's
been with this spinning head
it's not spinning
but I just feel like
I'm going to pass out any second

(step, step, step)

(deep gasp)

(step, step, step)

some more of it must have hit my system
through my nose or whatever

(step, step, step)

it's hard to concentrate on breathing

my heart is just like...

feeling really weird

my hands are getting numb

oh shit!

150

(deep exhale)

it's like as I started out
there is a part of me
that wants to stop
but there is a part of me
that has to get home

maybe I over exerted myself, I don't know

I walked kinda fast, I think

I feel like... (unrecognizable word)

(step, step, step)

it's nothing just now
it's like when I walked out, I uh...

and when all this shit started hitting me
just it's like when I walked around the building
I was just high...
then the minute I hit *the strand*
it was like over-powering
and 1 almost went down

(cough)

and it was like uh, unconscious,
I sniffed in really deep
and I thought
shit, I took in too much more of this shit
I got to quit doing it now
so I tried to pick my nose clean a little bit

(burp)

151

awh, cocaine burp
this is definitely the highest I have ever been
physically
not mentally

(step, step, step)

I guess this is like japan
and the poems I wrote that drunken night

it's funny my business manager kept,
keeps saying
what a fiasco that trip was for me financially
but it produced a book of poetry

so few ever understand art
how could that have bad?
no matter what the cost...

maybe this will be my last will and testament

(step, step, step)

(deep exhale)

(step, step, step)

(exhale)

(step, step, step)

a bicycle just went by

(step, step, step)

(unrecognizable ramblings)

152

(deep exhale)

I've never been so high like this before…

     (step, step, step)

     (sniff)

     (step, step, step)

     (exhale)

     (step, step, step)

almost at the end of *the strand* here
one more block

     (deep exhale)

     (vague talking by other people)

shit, two people just startled me
I hope that doesn't do in my heart

that adrenal rush

I don't know
it is really going to my head
my heart now

     (exhale)

walking back down and around
to hermosa avenue now

my heart hurts
hard to breathe

    (talking by other people)

the thing about valium is
I don't want to mix up drugs in my system
too much like that
take me down and out
I don't know

guess I'm just going to have to wait this out

I don't know

almost home

so I'm signing off here
I guess what comes, is what comes
and what ever does is all my fault
but...
as I say, if I die
at least I'll be free

interestingly enough my head doesn't even feel high
though I suppose

    (cough)

in retrospect I will think that I was
but I don't feel it

ah life
what a dance

    [taken from the tape, verbatim]

2

home
alive or dead
well, that is always a narrow margin
T.V. on
take my mind
take it from the pain
to the pain
take it anywhere
but where I am

3

2: A.M.
telephone call
the answering machine
2:03 A.M.
"well, fuck that, she must be home."
"I think I will try again."

"hello."
"hello."
"oh, it's you."
"how are you my L.A. scottish prince?"
"dying."
"did a bit too much cocaine."

        her story is lost
        as this semi-fine
        sweet young white bread
        type of thing, be

        crazy
        yeah, way over the deep end
        and I do mean literally
        not figuratively

        It was S.F.
        (san francisco), for the uninitiated
        a few days before
        at an exhibit opening
        she stared deeply into the lost realms
        of some painting
        that only she could see

        personally, truthfully

I thought that she was *dupped* up on
some acid with that distant and dilated
look in her eyes

well hey
I can play along

so we stared together
for an hour or so
then the museum closed
we were out-a-there
a walk on *the streets of san francisco*

like the T.V. show
remember?

then a bar

she had *dos* singapore slings

(don't get me thinking of asia)

me, I had *uno* mineral water

we then exchanged
in the magic of the moment
the most perfect first kiss of my life
then to her crib
then to a semi-serious sex session

"how's mr. cat?"
"you mean muffy?"
"whatever."

her fucking cat
spent the night

157

that night
the night I spent with her
continually waking me up
by trying to sleep on my face

as I told him
I was seriously thinking
of finding some hungry Vietnamese
in the area

"he, he's fine."
"he misses you."

in the morning, I awoke

(with the little sleep which I actually had
due to all the ongoing/on-feeling sex)

to, how shall I say
a rude awakening

her eyes
were just as distant
and her words
as tilted as the night before

anyway,
her insanity didn't bother me as much
as the violence she dished out
when I tried to bail
I mean real
      play misty for me
clint eastwood action

but that is all in some other piece of
literature

158

in some book
unwritten/not completed

in my vast library of things to do...

(a long story, made very short).

never will I see her again
never, never, never.

but then...
somewhere
in this lost cocaine O.D. session
somehow I felt a calling
a calling to call her
to make promises in the night
to know that there is willing love waiting

I had received, that day, monday
two, count them two
lost love letters from her

oh yeah, I had taken my uncle scotty's
advice,
> *"love them and leave 'em*
> *and don't give them your phone*
> *number."*

thus the letters

"will you come and see me? I need you. I want
     you. I want you. I love you."
"yes, tomorrow. if I'm still alive. I will come
     tomorrow. I will fly up there. I will rent
     a car. we will be together. I don't care if
     you're crazy."

"good night"
well alright

a moment lost from the pounding of my heart
the knots which it was trying to form

though my breath was short
periodic rushes to the brain
and a wonder
as to whether
I would indeed be alive
manana
if so, I had a date

> *a date I never kept*
> *letters that continue to come*
> *which I never answer*

dead or alive
life is all perception

in her mind
which am I

I really don't even care

4

T.V.
douses my mind
I flip through
the cable sent channels

a moment of this
a second of that
bad movies
bad T. V. shows
they all have become so predictable
they all have become so boring

5

my heart
it is alive
alive, on its own
"IT'S ALIVE!"
I want to scream
I, on the other hand,
am in perpetual question

6

do I say, "never again?"
like on one of those
one too many
wake up in the morning
hangover sessions
no
I do not
alive or dead
what a way to go
hold the art tight
hold it with a reason
hold it with a vengeance
and die
in its artistic arms

O.D.
or suicide
a far better way to go
than at the hands
of some foolish
disease
that you have no control over

    (a disease like age)

7

3:00 A.M.
time to talk again
give me a reason
to hold on to reality
telephone in hand
dial the number
three rings
and *nada*

my sweet little
japanese
former rich girl
former babe
now a bit overweight
nuisance
who calls me and calls me
twice, three times a day
every day
wanting a date
but no, I want a dream
not a date
and one worth living
one worth feeling
one worth taking a chance with and for
but now
now...
you can serve a purpose
a purpose past the one you served
upon our meeting
what was it,
yes, three years ago

no answer
no purpose

you served nothing

three rings
I know you are home
but I do not wish
to wake your aging parents
so three rings is it
bye-bye
to a hello
which 1 never received

8

life
its destiny
its call
it definitely
called me out tonight

9

am I alive
am I dying
well, in truth
who can ever really say
who ever really know

my heart
yes, my heart, it still knots
my breath
well, I am breathing
my head
down for hours or more

cocaine
the goddess
cocaine
the life
and how it slips out of our grasp
so easily
I love it

I love to feel
I love to live

just sometimes
I wish that living
felt a wee bit better

10

three hours
passed and plus the walk
alive?
well, more or less

I'm going to live
live through it
this time anyway

the light is coming out
coming up

I guess I will go to bed

11

5:45 A. M.
my telephone rings
international call
I hear the static
on the line

"malaysia calling dr. scott shaw."
"yes."
"is this dr. scott shaw?"
"yes."
"malaysia calling."

> a bit redundant there,
> aren't you babe

"hello scott... hello..."
"yes."

> now to shorten the convo
> and the statement of fact
> it was my babe
> one of my babes
> K. L.
> (kuala lumpur, for the uninitiated)
> on the line
> from the line
> malaysia
> it had been two weeks
> since I was there
> since I saw her last

"my sister is dying of cancer."
"then she will be free."
"how can you say that, scott?"

"she had it and never told anyone."
"be happy for her. she will be free."
"how, can you say that, just how can you say
that."
"because I am here dying. dying from too much
cocaine. I want no one to cry any tears over me. I
want them to be happy."
"you can't die! I love you scott."
"so."
"all my friends say that I'm a fool. they tell me
you have women all over the world. they tell me
you say, *I love you,* to all of them. they tell me
to forget you."
"they are right."

        now to abbreviate a half hour plus convo
        into its shortest possible application
        she *rap'd* on about her sister
        I told her there was nothing that she
        could do
        she was worried about me
        I told her if I died
        to be happy because then I would be free

"bye, bye."

I had hung up
before she had the opportunity
to sufficiently, (to her standards)
tell me how worried she was of and for me

I tried to chill back
and catch some Z's

RING!

170

"malaysia calling dr. scott shaw."
"yes."
"is this dr. scott shaw?"
"yes."

  good, she wasn't redundant this time

"scott! are you OK?"
"just see me in the wind."

  as I hung up
  I could hear her scream

"WAIT!"

play it
play it full on
live it
bring the melodrama to life
breathe it
to the maximum

and finally I went to sleep

12

I definitely cracked a piston on this one
well, I have cracked them before
the only problem is
that I do not have many more to crack
before it is down for the count

not the standing eight
like this sweet session

but down for the big one
ten on the canvas

so I say,
dream on dreamers

live on

feel on

what ever the price is
pay it

for living empty
with no experience to show for it
is a far worse fate
than to die at the hands
of a momentary high

13

Last Will and Testament

and to you I leave
my bad little '64 porsche 356 sc
I always promised it to you anyway
it has a personality crisis at the moment
it is still in the shop
so you, you can pick up the tab

and I leave to you my guitar collection
do what you must
do what you will with it/with them
but remember they are all works of art
and most you will never see again

and I leave you all of my paintings
the ones I did
the ones you did
even the ones I have purchased
for who else do I know
who else have I ever known
that would/that could
ever appreciate art
as you have/as you do

as well, I leave you all my poetry
and all of my other written works
including my journals

please try to understand the space I was in
when I wrote many of the things that I said

I guess that's it
I guess I leave you everything

no one else even matters
no one else ever has

I leave you everything
everything but my debts
them, I cast to the realms
of the checked out
dying and dead of unpaid,
no way to collect
never-never-land
bye-bye-ville
to the credit card companies
unpaid, dollars lost forever, bills

but all else
my cameras
my bicycles
my library
my records, cd's, etc.

all to you
for who else has ever known me better
who else has known me more
all to you
my main L.A. babe
my forever L.A. lady
who I have not even seen
in such a long time
the joke is
I do not even know where you are
we have lost each other in the wind
the winds of time
the winds of change
but I will leave that to the attorneys
that's the gift
I leave to them

174

to find you
and give you all my worldly possessions
where ever it is
that you may be
what ever it is
that they may be worth

and mostly I give you
an eternal loving kiss, goodbye
and a sorry for all the hell
I put your through
a sorry for the me, being me
you were too good
to have lived through that
the me, being me
hopefully this will pay you back
in some small way

14

as the seventh day
comes to a close
I am still not
one-hundred percent on
this bad boy
definitely did
take me for a ride

a knot in my heart
here or there

a day or two of separated and spaced vision

      but distance is a dream
      a dream to the underachieved
      distance holds a key
      unlocking the necessity
      to not accomplish anything

      my journey jetlag
      is curing
      my heart, well...
      it probably will heal

      and the session
      now it is
      for the record
      for the fools like I
      who find poetry in the wind
      and experience
      at the gates of death

      dream on...

seven days later and I'm still alive...

S.
88.27.6
Redondo Beach, California

Chapter 5

On the Hard Edge
of Hollywood

1

I guess it all started in '69
'69, moved from south-central L.A. to hollywood
an apartment on harold way
a dirty little side street
off of hollywood and normandie
lined with some 1960's style square
       apartment buildings
some 1940's houses
losing their lost way in the lost world
       of rapid change
I was eleven
the hippie *thAng* was full on
I'd walk down the boulevard and see dudes
eyes *tripp'n* deep,
lost into the realms of some vision
unseen/unknown
       L-S-D
I'd walk the streets because
there was really nothing better to do
the deep hot summer, full on
AM radio blasting pop rock n' roll
new kid on a kid-less street
no one to talk to
except the old dreamers with no passion left to feel
too old to know that it was too late
too late to be left alive
eleven years old
I walked among them
the hippies and the old poets
seeking a reason/my reason
dreaming of all the things a 1969 kid dreams about
but, instead I was handed:
white cross, jones, and acid
never dreaming I'd live so long

to be smashing hard into the realms of the
one of them
the too longed lived
but, here I am twenty-five plus years later
running from hollywood
but, hollywood chases me
hollywood is never too far away

2

music pounds hard
rhythmic movement
I got a drink in my hand
but, the music
it makes me want to dance

red light
dead center, pouring into my eyes
it almost blinds my sight
like a camera flash/like the sun

passing in front of it
moving as if moving meant something
the red light
it, momentarily is blocked
I see the vision
the vision is clear
her form, an ancient dance
slithering like a snake about to strike
a python, ready to kill

a chrome bar, passes up to the ceiling
a chrome bar
like a fireman would slide down
she, she moves up to it
wraps her legs around it
making love to it/she embraces it
spinning into a sexual frenzy
on a chrome pole
       hard, very hard
       steel hard
       like no real man
       could ever stay

in her spinning
her eyes meet mine

she slides down
down off of the pole

movement
her body lays down on the floor
she spreads her legs
her pelvis raises up
down/up/down/up
she fucks the air

I pull a dollar bill out of my pocket
I put a dollar bill into my mouth
I walk up to the stage
eye to eye
I slowly remove it from my lips
sliding it from side to side
I lick it
I lay it on the bars surrounding her

bars to keep me out
bars to keep her in
I don't know

she smiles/I smile
a dollar spent
a dance done
it all means nothing

another dollar on a promises illusion
which will never happen

184

3

the lights smash down hard
on the drunken head
of a drunken man
attempting to find mysticism
in the hands of lust
at the hands of excess
surrounded by fools
the fools of the world
who drink only to drink
heredity/psychology/escape

       but, escape to where?
       I've always pondered
       escape to why?
       the question remains

a seedy club
on the wrong side of hollywood
they pour their watered down beer
out of the tap/into a glass
a promised illusion of nothingness

I sit among them/the fools
fools like me
we all have our reasons for being here
the reasons all equal the same thing

nothing

4

night time - promised passion
the pacifier of dreams
we, venchenzo and me, sit
in a semi sleazy hollywood bar
smalls
a little place over on the non-fag side
of santa monica boulevard

it's almost christmas
they've strung a bunch of christmas tree lights
across the ceiling

      it's very bright in here
            very light
      when it is usually very dark

      very light
      too much to be seen
      in a room with not
      too much worth looking at

we got here early
we got one of the two booths

we sit back
my back leans against the brick wall
we continue our wetting of lips

      drink

we smoke some cuban cigars
seeking a vision
worth visualizing
in a bar-room filling

186

with the too old to know any better
the too young that still think this place is cool

and, I guess I just never learned the rules
too restless to ever really care

and, I guess they say jesus is a savior
but, you can't be saved
when you just don't believe

so, here I sit
across the table from venchenzo
one of the. . .
no, two of the damned

two, who just never cared enough to care
two, who never attempted to believe the lie

we sit
we watch
we laugh at the joke engulfing our presence
people/saturday night
thinking they are/pretending they are
one of us
one of the damned

I look/I see
it is obvious they are not
they still believe

5

venchenzo and I go back
twenty, twenty-five years deep or so
another hollywood kid with a mind full of dreams
and a world smashing down
way too hard
to ever dig his way out enough
to live any of them

him and me
two down *mutha' fuckers*
coming straight out of the ghetto
noth'n left to lose

he came up over by hollywood and western
up the street from the *saint francis hotel*
they've shot movies there
junky/whores/murderers
they all made it their home

they always shoot movies on our old turf
some people even dream to live on those dirty
violent streets

>   badlands in a bad world
>   a fool's desire

>   thus for, and as such
>   him and I
>   venchenzo and me
>   we go out
>   OUT
>   to lose our selves deep into the night

188

deep into the dark
        deep into the drink
and the various other forms of intoxication

    seeking vision
        seeking solace
           seeking forgiveness
seeking something/anything more than nothing

that's what this tail is all about

and, if you haven't been there
you could never know
don't even think about going there
it's never what it seems

6

night smashes hard
against the dripping illusion of hollywood
nothingness
and I go out onto the streets -- AGAIN

seeking a cure -- which is non-existent
seeking the miracles -- which never seem to come
but, still I go

we walk down cahuenga B-L-V-D
intensions on *the burgundy room*

we, ken-dog, and I go inside
small, dark, smoky

like, you know, the style
all the places depicted
in all those 1940 hollywood movies

back when smoking was cool
back before it was revealed the smoke
KILLED you dead
back before it was told the tobacco companies
were messing with nicotine levels
        to addict faster
        to suck you in
        to kill you harder

        die -- in a deathful way

           speaking of. . .

it was dead inside
dead, in the way only hollywood dead could be

190

filled to the brim with neo-hip hollywood types

      goatees
      dudes, hair shaved tight
      chicks - died platinum blonde
      retro bell bottoms

      we walk out

now I'm hang'n tonight with this guy
met him maybe fives years back
doing a film
when I was an evil drug dealing - killer - co-star
he was an asian drug kingpin

back in the days when I was a bad actor
but, I got a lot of roles

back when my long hair
was considered cool
back when my very baggy suits
for a moment
were the trend
             back then

now, a relative good actor
and. . .

anyway, me and he/he and me - we went on
made a few films together
got some not bad reviews
but made no money

he's got a job
me, I still make the movies

we walk across the streets
jay-walk cahuenga B-L-V-D
we notice people walking down
        the alley way-backside
"let's go take a look."

we walk passed a bum
like a guardian into the abyss-full realms of the
deathful nothing
posted at the side of empty parking lot
guarding nothing but his lifeless life
guarding the realms which only too few
could ever experience
guarding, as if it all matter
but, it doesn't

we walk
past where the lights fade to a dull glow
past where there are any other people

desolate - cold - old - dying hollywood

        sounds almost poetic
        believe me, it's not

up inside another smoky bar
people crowd together
way too much
way too much for each other

any other place
any other time
they would never even want
to be so close
to the equally hollywood stylish
equally hollywood trendy

192

goatees
cigarettes
dr. martin boots

grabbed a couple budweiser from the bar maid
nothing really left to do
nothing, for sure, left to loose

bam! one hit
mine, in was gone
pass me another, if you please

in my left ear, I'm hearing the meaningless chatter
of the meaningless masses
in my right ear
a dude way to close
exclaims to his friend,
"If you carry a gun, that only means you are waiting
for the time to kill someone."

waiting, I think
as if it hasn't already happened
a time, no two, no three
I mean fuck,
this is L.A.

I laugh to myself

me, I'm strapped
I look down at my ankle
a glock held tight

I look over at my partner
his waistline
underneath his coat
glock

gats

a bullet and the city
hollywood
and this one's got your name on it *mutha' fucker*
right between the eyes

finish our beers
we leave
this bar
way too cool for us.

7

I remember this one time
I'd been sitting on a gram or three of *caine*
I'd do a solo line here/a solo line there
but, this night -- saturday night
alone, too alone
no one to call/no one who wanted to hear it

I banged down a line
nostril right
banged down a line
nostril left
times ten, fifteen, twenty -- I don't know. . .

I was ON/I was wired

OUT -- called
but where was out?

solo
is always so god damned HARD

anyway, I got in my jeep -- top off
dead of winter
wearing this long, east coast style coat I own
its brown -- kinda

I drove. . .
drove south down *pacific coast highway*
deep into the reaches of long beach -- *the LBC*
where the cambodian whores exist
if you know where to find 'em
where the *gang bangers* dwell
maximum violence

I've always preferred the seedy
the low
the rundown
somehow I feel safer there

anyway, back to the storyline at hand. . .

wired on the *caine*
living the heaven only cocaine can make you feel

though my world had been falling down around me
no one/no thing/no care

BAM -- I was cured
cocaine -- the cure

I once had this chick
my once-upon-a-time, main L.A. babe
fucked up head, maximum

we lined up one day
"shit, why don't they make this stuff legal," she said
"it would cure a lot of depressed people."
"no shit. . . and, addict a lot more," I added

a reason for larceny
a reason for violence
a reason to kill

but, that was then, a long time ago
a time long before this. . .

but me, I drove through the gutters
caine pounding in my brain
"IT'S ALL GOING TO BE OKAY -- ALRIGHT."
instant cure, at the hands of a drug

196

so I hit the seedy side/the dark side
where all the dweller of the night
embrace their unique brand of mysticism

I drive/I see
a cambodian darling
pacing the pathways of the night

> I drive by once
> she looks
> I drive by twice
> she smiles
> I drive by a third time
> she gets in

now, I've watched *cops* on T.V.
        way too many times
and where the fuck there are hookers for $20.00
damned if I will ever find out

this is L.A., long beach, south of hollywood
and a *scag-hoe*
walking the street
wants $100.00 minimum to clean my plumbing

        seemed like a fair price to pay. . .

the night time sky looked fine
as I stared up from my jeep
I stared into the sky
saw the few remaining stars
that the L.A./LBC smog lets you see

I lay back
I look up
my back laying on my reclined seat

she was on top of me
in control of the action
my mind on cuming/on her/on this moment
on hoping the cops/or some *bangers* don't drive by
and interrupt our session

occasionally I glanced at her
pretty
I could have loved her
once upon a time
now
her life/like mine
way to gone to ever be known
way too much knowledge
of the kind that no one else can know
no one else can understand

       I call it
       the enlightenment of the street
       it takes a long time to find
       a lot longer to know
       but once you know
       you know
       and it is something so few cold ever grasp.

our enlightenment met with our merged bodies
my dick planted deeply into her
on the streets of the late night
LBC

8

walking though a midnight parking lot
out of the corner of my eye
I see this girl
passing
the other way

        she
        she sees me

        she stares
        I know those eyes

now, what has it been
ten years
no more like fifteen

a one time dream
a one time lover
of a one time fantasy

once upon a one time
that I thought would last forever

should have/could have/did not

in thinking back
I am so glad
I walked when I walked
back then
way back then

psycho bitch
you know the one
every poet writes about her

but hot
she was hot

dyed black hair
dyed black heart
bright red lips
chinese eyes
could fuck
like there was no tomorrow

I see her
I see her see me

I know
I remember
but, I keep my walk
walking on

that night/then
I go and get my drink on
waltz back to my ride
I drive
having forgotten the vision
of what I had seen/her
a couple of hours the previous

I drive
       hop the freeway
       405 south

I drive
I get off
a little hold up in one lane
the one lane
over to my right

200

up next to me
pulls a car
a car I had never seen before
I glance
another glance
a third glance out of
the corner of my eyes

like the one before
earlier that evening

I glance
and there she is
a vision of remembrance
remembrance for the second time

she has followed me
tried to follow me home
tried to find out where I live
discover what went wrong
try to live the love again
try to haunt my dreams
one more time

ten
no fifteen
fifteen years later

I look
I see
I take the opportunity
I jam off
turn left
when I want to turn right

run
as she is tied up
tied in the one-lane
that has traffic problems

I drive
I think
I realize
people never change

not her/not I
not the what should have been
that moment
hers and mine
that span two years

but, her silent chase
it has left me with the question
a remembrance
of what should never have been
but was

I question
should I just have smiled
said, "hi."
and reentered the nightmare

9

she was a beautiful little creature
nisei
japanese princess

she earned her wage
playing mini-mouse
over disneyland way

we met
when I was casting a movie
at a coffee house
over on beverly blvd.
west hollywood

long black hair
eyes that kissed the night
and she loved me

me -- too
I fell in loved with her

we did
what you do in hollywood
        when love is fresh
        when love is new

we got in on guest-lists
saw friends who were in bad-bands
        playing bad music
        dreaming of stardom

we made love on the beaches
in the back seats of cars

didn't need to
didn't have to
it is/was
just the perfection of the moment
        the lost space in time
            when the new love is all that matters
            when the new love is the promise
            that will take you away from the night

one day
over at a friend's music shop
a shop where I get my guitars made/tuned up
a guy
a bass player that I knew
made his wage playing
on one of disneyland's stages
"you know her?"
"you're going out with her?"
"man, I have had fantasies about that girl!"

        and life it is a fantasy
        a fantasy
        you have to live

        live for life
        for it is all that we have
        for it is all that we know

        live to live
        because what else is there

the girl
I gave her a part in a movie
her first staring role
I gave her a part
but there was the problem

204

I was working with a guy on the film
letting him ride my wave
he claimed/pretended
to be my friend
she had the chance to talk to him
that was my mistake

she ask the wrong questions
to the wrong guy

he told her I was a vampire
a creature who prowled the streets
deeply hidden in the night

a touch/a kiss
drink the blood
take what any woman has to give me
then I would be gone
lost into the night
the girl left holding her heart
in her hand

true to some/if not many degrees
but it is all how the stories are told

the girl got scared
she ran away

so, lost
was that chance to see what happened
and I will never know
what it may have equaled
stolen by the words
the hidden jealousies
of a so-called friend
and you never what you never know

years later
I sat near the beach
eating lunch
with this so-called friend

he tells me
his life ended
when I stopped making movies with him
when I stopped
inviting him along for the ride

I smile
I remembered
I go home
and write these words
about a part of my life ended
when I was betrayed

a part of my life that was not allowed to play out
and I will never know
what I will never know

so lost
so long ago
that girl
in a dream
I remember how
we made love
on a nighttime beach

10

venchenzo calls me up
about twelve
in the noon o'clock
"hey, what's up, man?"
"you want to go and waste some more money and
some more time."
"noth'n to loose but my life, my man. I'm there."

so, I hit over to his crib
down venice way

early, on an early start
"yeah, we may as well drink all day," I said

but the life time
turns into the night time
and I can't help but wondering where the time has
gone

yeah, I know
years in asia
years lost in day dreams
equaling little
on the equaling scale
but then, what does life really equal - anyway

venchenzo and me
we were doing this same thing a decade back

he questions our, "why"

"we never got old," I answer
"never had a reason to."
"never had kids."

"never had house payments."
"never had some chick
		telling us we had to stop behaving this way."

all good or bad
I just know
your call

post a basketball game on the T.V.
post a dozen beers each
post a bottle of the grape, maybe two
time to take life to the life-line
time to hit the streets

hollywood
the rainbow

back when venchenzo and I were punks
PUNKS in the stylistic side of the word
that place used to be a joke
then came the re-made/re-do
late 1980's heavy metal craze
and. . .
for what ever fool's reason
we went -- THERE -- upon occasion
I guess nothing better to do

now, deep in the 1990's
lost in a city with no direction
a jungle of purpose with no style

every now and then
we dig *the rainbow* out of the places
we every-time claim
"NEVER AGAIN"

inside on a neon filled saturday night
the dudes with hair still teased
up way too high
the chicks with skin tight vinyl pants
and spike heels

I just don't understand how people can get lost
in an era
which *ain't never com'n back*

inside
post a pound down of a dozen drinks or so
the dance floor is pick'n up
we strut our bad self's down there
venchenzo and I

post your basic eye contact I move in and on
with this six month here
japanese
out-a-tokyo chick

oh yeah, did I mention
a lot of japanese chicks tend to hang there
you know, the japanese *thAng* for americans
rock n' roll and all. . .

as mentioned, I move in and on
to this female of a not even nearly nearing
semi fine babe
who dances, like all asian chicks seem to do
badly and into the mirror

personally I don't get it
kinda like jack'n off, I guess
but, I just don't want to watch myself dance
hell, or watch myself jack off for that matter. . .

so, I get my grove on with her
slide in between the mirror and her-self

just for the record
it is, however, god damned hard
to get your rhythm on
to some late 1980's head bang'n band

anyway. . .

venchenzo tries to move in
on her straight out of the tokyo back streets friend
he slices his soul-full self up tight on her
way too tight, I guess
she wasn't ready to play
she pushes him back
"fuck you," he yells
punches a wall
walks off and gets another drink

me, no passion with a purpose
the chick apparently dig'n my scene
I move on/in/closer/tighter

the dancing fades into the never-never
I look over
venchenzo relocated himself
he's got this black chick
tight up against the wall
he's sliding up and down her form

she's obviously more responsive
he's got a drink in one hand
her ass in the other
moving with all his best white boy/soul-full moves

210

venchenzo and I
kinda strange, I guess
like my shrink tells me
white on the out side
but inside I see myself as black

I don't know
I guess my formative years
growing up on the wrong side of the tracks
down south-central L.A. way
only white boy
in an all black school

first girl I slapped lips with
black
I was five years old
I still remember the feeling of her buck teeth
plastered against my mouth

I move/venchenzo moves
all hoping for something more than nothing
a touch/a feel/a kiss/a fuck

venchenzo's dancing left of me
I look, I guess the drink called him out
more then the chick
with out a word
he leaves her dancing solo
she watches his movement
as he walks from the dance floor

she doesn't known what to do

he does that
when he needs a drink

he just picks up and walks away
no word/no sound/no look

she
the girl
the sweet soul sister
retreats with her solo moves
up against the wall
she sways as the hard rock pounds

me, I'm still locked up with the hoped for
promised passion
dancing
when up walks with these two dude
way longed haired with bangs
cowboy boots, tight black pants, leather jackets
you know the type.
losers. . .

they, especially the one
apparently knows my latched into
fresh off the boat
japanese chick
he talks to her

now, this goes on for a moment or three
I scan my mind
there is a couple of ways I could handle this
situation

one, bail

no, can't do that

two, go and move with
venchenzo's black soul sister

212

show the chick, I just don't care

no, can't do that either
can't *dis* my friend

option three
which I choose

I reach my arm out
wrap it around the guy's neck
I pull him in tight to me
all smiles, I say,
"if you don't get the fuck out of here immediately
      I am going to take your fuck'n ass out of the
      picture right here, right now."

I let go
I smile at him
I smile at the girl
he looks at me
scared
and leaves

I dance on

post, the previous
venchenzo reemerges
new drink in his hand
walks up to the black chick
begins to move as if he had never left

the night goes on
we, venchenzo and me, drive home -- solo
a telephone number in my pocket
a telephone number
which I will never call

11

I was teaching this university class
on filmmaking

      class overloaded

with egos
with wanta be filmmakers
with dykes
with idiots
with idiot dykes
with exchange students

      wanting only a visa
      to live close to
      hollywood

with a porn filmmaker
armenian *gangsta*

      why he took the class
      it was always a surprise
      to me

now the last night of the class
he invites me out
we go to *down* hollywood
strip club way

we hit *jumbo's*
old school hollywood

we hit *cheetas*
new school hollywood

214

now
>
> if I have any advice to give you
> it would be
> to go out to a strip club
> with an armenia *gangsta*

but post the advice
back to the story at hand

the night rained
in its rock n' roll visions
as the music pounds
and the girls dance on their poles

nights known
way too many times to count

I notice a girl
a dancer
a one time b-movie star
I put her in a movie once
once, a long-long time ago

she dances
no one seems to care
I go up to the stage
a ten dollar bill
stuck between my lips
I lick it

> *It's just my way. . .*

I place it
in front of her

I smile

as I think back to the one time fantasy
the fantasy I had about her
so, so long ago. . .

now, here she dances
alone on a stage
older, much older
older, like I
and the fantasy
it is all gone

I place the money on the stage
I smile
I turn
I walk away

I was the only one
who cared enough
to toss a dime
how sad was that

I didn't see her
the dance
the one-time b-movie queen
the rest of that night
what I did see
was lap dance after lap dance
paid for by the house
paid for with the sweat of the girls
paid for by a student
from a class
armenia *gangsta*
armenia porn filmmaker
a class I taught
over
university extension way

we congregate back at the table
my student, the girls, and I

"I almost came," he exclaims
"wow, that is serious
            premature ejaculation," I thought

but more importantly
one girl
she was in love

she was jealous of the
gorgeous
blonde
wanta-be
actress
who licked my face
touched my body
and rubbed my dick
for an eternity

            eternity
            in terms of the strip club world

she really should have stayed in idaho
this dance/this dream

because hollywood
is no place for anybody

all you end up to be is
a stripper/a hooker/a dreamer

            a dreamer
            of dreams that can never be

but, this girl
a dance
not the dancer
another dancer
she was jealous
she had impatiently
awaited my return

she wanted me
for me
me for her
her for now
now forever

      she was alright in her own way
      do-able, I guess

      long dark hair
      big spanish eyes

      do-able
      for lack of anything better to do

now most people go to strip clubs
believing that they can get laid
but it never happens
at least not for most
stripper are not hooker
at least they are not hookers yet

strippers
are believers
they think that tomorrow
mr. right
is going to walk through that door

mr. right
will come in
and save them from hell

and for some reason
strippers love me
I guess
they think
I am that mr. right
how wrong they are
I always get the invite
          out/later

but this night/that night
I had my student
he was my age
looked way older
he was too fucked up to drive
so I got the girls digits
he
my student and I
jumped in his range rover
I drove us down to *sam woo's*
in chinatown
to get our grub on
got him back to his pad

4:00 A.M.
I make a telephone call
on the cell
one more mr. right
who is not
one more night with a girl
and I do not even remember her name

welcome to hollywood

12

a night
a night club

venchenzo gets up to hit the head
I lay back in the cut
listing to some new wave pop
from the early 1980's
playing over the sound system
yeah, I was there,
          then

my eyes scan
for any possible signs of promised passion
a female with a willing glance
I see nothing
nothing, at least worth my attention

I look over and see the line forming
at the men's head
the door is open
I see venchenzo sitting on the toilet
not shitting/just sitting
he's gone down hard
on a day
with just too many flavors of alcohol

he sits/I watch
I've got his back

waiting for any wanta-be asshole
to break fly with him
give him some shit
give me a reason/a moment
to liven up the night

to go and take somebody/some asshole out

but, they're all nothing
the wait like fool's
standing
waiting
for a guy sitting on a toilet
to fucked up to stand up
I wait for some action
there is none

13

a lot of people lie to the themselves
tell themselves that it all means something
something as opposed to nothing
something on the nothing scale

      jobs
      family
      cars
      houses
      credit cards

      payments
      to pay for a something

      me, I prefer to just get drunk

14

the evening begins
as they begin
I hop over to 711
in hermosa
grab a big - bad
super jumbo sized java
three mini creams
three mini mochas
        additives added

I drive down
the p.c.h.
hit venice
hit venchenzo's

we pop down a dozen
cans of the elixir
hit the night
hit the hollywood
where there is sill
one remaining
gothic underworld club
worth going to

we go
we enter
walk pass the girl
collecting dollars at the door

I smile
I wave
I never pay

inside, it is pounding
pounding it all its darkness

dark to light
light to night
the secret realm of screams
known only to the knowers

two girls sitting solo
we go and make convo

I mean
no one else was

they looked far
distant
not in the right place
not in the right space
                    of time
                    or mind

we talk
we drink
we get further
fucked up
we go back to venchenzo's crib
back by the venice beach

inside,
my girl
interested
we go into the bathroom
my hand in the pudding
her tongue down my throat
she is pulling down my zipper

when I hear,
"slut!"
"slut!"
"you're a slut!"

her friends voice rings out

      obviously venchenzo wasn't getting any...

so story told
her friend throws
the major
          cock
          block

she
the girl
my girl
 says she is sorry
says she will call me in the AM

it turns out
she only lives a few blocks from me
down on the beach
soutbay

the girls they leave
we
venchenzo and I
sit in the absolute
of zero
we drink
like only
true broken friends can do

yes, we are the damned
two of the damned

another night
another dream stolen

I go home
I go to sleep
a call in the AM
the girl wants to pick up
where we left off

but any night illusion
is never worth seeing
in the day
where the effects of the goddess drink
have faded
and what could have been
never came to be

this is hollywood.

15

we're out
out the door
grab a couple of *two-fours* for the road
we drink 'em *en route*
dance club
no action
we leave
120 miles an hour
my
'64 porsche 356 sc
down the freeway
I don't remember why
blacked out
but I do remember the gage
120 miles an hour

they always say you know your an alcoholic
when you have black outs

I think somebody wanted to race me
they lost

we go to a strip club
new vietnamese chick
she does a table dance
she's raw
rubs her bar pussy on my forehead
yeah
we go home
do
what
I can't remember
what

sleep it off
a night to be reassured of the nothingness

I did something
I did someone
I just don't remember
who/what

16

friday
traffic
major traffic
on the 405 south bound

my wheels rumble under me
the freeway in need of repair

dead Stop
all Stop
non Stop

the city
people of the city
going somewhere to nowhere
nowhere to nothing

something always ends up equaling nothing

and, where do I go in this mass of confusion
me, seeking illusion
obsessing about the obsess-able
dreaming of another desire
another place
another time
anther illusion to allow my body to fall into

embraced
sucked in
drowned in the love
the lust

and, in the end
that too

will all mean nothing
but the nothing which means something

the nothing which equals something else

the radio plays songs from the 1980s

the 1980s
a decade ago
a musical era ago
where did it all go

>   a decade
>   ten years
>   a lifetime
>   gone, spent, lived, lost

a dream of a memory
the memory of being in some stranger's arms

and I remember her
only for a moment

only as superficially as a memory can be
remembered

it was her, bangkok
a decade ago

and, her memory tosses me into the wonder
the wonder of why I am here, L.A.
traffic
traffic-jammed

the wonder of why I am not there, bangkok
where all the dreams are so close at hand

230

17

this girl
she asks to be in one of my movies

a fine little
       wonder white bread *thAng*
                out of texas

"I'll take my top off"
       she tell me

I smile
       "you don't have to take your top off.
       at least not in the movie."

then we go out
we go to have a drink
we drink a lot
I mean, the girl could drink
kept up with me
round-for-round

she was looking for new meaning
came out here to L.A.
to find just that
me, I was looking for a new lie
another lie in the passion

       where, as it has been for years
       any dream will do

it all came together
her/and I
perfection in the making

almost perfect
almost time
but have you ever meant one thing
      yet said another
words that just did not come out right
I did that
      to her
over the telephone line

a joke
      came out like an insult
I didn't really mean it that way

so what could have been
      never was/never happened

I don't know
maybe it was the gods of destiny
saving me
from some cruel
and heartless fate
maybe it was just payback
payback for all the babes
I walked away from
left before
anything
was ever allowed to happen

but here it is for the memory
here it is for the chance
here it is for what never happened
here it is for the dream
that should have been lived

      but now it is all too late
        I wish I remembered her name

18

I'm forty-four years old
I have a twenty year old
girl friend

twenty years old
and in love with me

I try to remember
call up from the dark ages
recapture
how it feels
to be in love
at twenty

I can think about it
it is like an old forgotten movie

      distant
      faded
      remembered
      but gone

love
infatuation
that totality of creation

that
all that matters
dream

that fantasy
of forever

I think
I remember
but
I can not feel that way anymore
      how sad is that?

I have long wanted to
dive back in
dream the dreams
of my youth
recapture
what was taken
what is gone/what is lost

hold on to the dream
for just one more sessions

      that flame
      that got blown out
          somewhere/sometime
      when
      I do not know
      but gone
      it is gone

      can it be relighted?

so again
I am cast off to the dream
a new dream to feel
I am forty-four
I have a twenty year old
girlfriend

      twenty years old
      and she is in love with me

234

19

I have one babe
      a hot
      little latina lover

      young
      she is very young

she waits at home
waits by the telephone
waits for me to call

she begs me
to take her out

      out and away
      but home by ten
      she has curfew

I have another babe
tall and lean
from the right
side of the tracks

      rich/beijing

I sit here
in a coffee house
santa monica
waiting

      waiting
      to forget
      the promise of passion

waiting
to forget the dream

waiting
to lose the desire

waiting
for the choice to come

I try to forget
that I have a desire
but, I can not
the choice is made
I go to my young
latina love

20

fading off into the distance
I look
I walk away

    gone
    distant
    removed
    never to be seen again

    fading…

I sit
I wonder
how many times that has happened
that perfect vision/that perfect girl

    our eyes meet
    we like what we see

    I like her/she likes me

    we smile
        we think
            we wonder

    how to make contact
        but then the time is gone

    she walks/I walk

    our moment of chance is gone

    separated for eternity
    the moment

the look
the lost of possible love
the loss of probable lust
it is lost to the possibility of eternity
forever

lost/gone

left only to the words
written upon a page

the only trace
of a memory
a memory of what
should have/could have
happened

21

I guess it is the curse of age

      time ticking
      time watching
      hating to waste even one moment

I guess it is the curse of age
wanting all moments
to equal something more

      be more

but this moment
this time
can only be lost

this hour of wanting
can never be repaired

      funny
      how many hours of my life
      have been spent
      sitting
      speaking of the illusion
      writing of the living

      living a life
      that so few have chosen to know

            most
            want homes
            want families
            want the promise of a promise

thanks
but no thanks

not for me
thank you very much
no thanks

     seeking the dream
     holding onto the lies

     and the female liars
     they always lie

just like life
just like the promises
of the promised

those who hold onto faith

     belief
     the church
     the illusion of forever
     in heaven
     as long as they
     follow the rules on earth

rules
who made those rules up anyway

why are we suppose to want
all the zero
that promised nothing

     but heartache
     work
     humiliation

bowing to the needs
and desires
of others

why is that suppose to be so good

a dream of a night
waiting to happen

a moment lived
in all of its illusion

a kiss
hello

a kiss
goodbye

at least it was
a moment/a life

lived…

22

sweet little/sweet *thAng*
lives in *the val*
the val via L.A. via taipei

sweet
with an edge

      a porno edge
      wants to do porno style things

      looks can be deceiving…

short
little
short hair
tiny

asks me, "what kind of girl do I look for?"
"oh, you'll do just fine," I answer

fine she does/fine she is
a moment/moment(s)
cast to the darkness of eternity
cast to the suchness of reason
giving me a moment to believe
      if only for a moment

      a moment is just fine with me

we go out
hit a bar here or there
at the beach

she drives us there

has this very expensive
european sport car

"let's put the top down.'

drive and drink
I've done it so many time before

looking for something/lost in the nothing

    the drink
    the girl
    the beach
    the wind blowing through my hair

drink done
we're a little fuck up
we closed out that bad little bar

drink done
love to me made
we walk
hand-in-hand
down to the water

drink done
we make love in the sand

    perfect like all perfect loves should be
    lived for a moment
    but remember for a lifetime
    we did make some serious love
    down on the sand

3:00 A.M
maybe 4:00

I'm wired/not tired
the pantry
got to get my eats on

so we drive downtown
among the hallowed/the hollowed
the lost to the night

>how many time
>for how many years
>have I gotten my grub on
>here/there
>deep in the realms of the night

her
not like me
she sleeps
sprawled across the table

the waiter laughs
I laugh at him
laughing at me
laughing at her

>a perfect moment
>in a perfect paradise

after the eats
she goes home/I go home
I see the sun
as it illuminate the ocean

framing/outlining
my home

evening, next
see her again
she states
"I'm sore. you are so big."

I smile as I walk away
she is so small

it could have been one of those things
one of those things
that you dream about
one of those things
that last forever

but
it was not

for when so much perfection is lived
in so short a time
all that can occur
is down hill from here/from there

I saw her
later
she questioned, "why'd you break up with me."

"I didn't break up with you.
        I just didn't want to damage the perfection."

        let the perfection
        the memory of the perfection

                last a lifetime

www.ingramcontent.com/pod-product-compliance
Lightning Source LLC
Chambersburg PA
CBHW060018100426
42740CB00010B/1522